Bow Wow TAO

Wit, Wisdom, and Dogma

BY CHU TOY

Voyageur Press

Edited by Kari Cornell
Designed by Julie Vermeer
Printed in China

05   06   07   08   09   5   4   3   2   1

Library of Congress Cataloging-in-Publication Data

Toy, Chu.
  Bow wow Tao : wit, wisdom, and dogma / by Chu Toy.
    p. cm.
  ISBN-13: 978-0-89658-713-7 (hardback)
  ISBN-10: 0-89658-713-4 (hardback)
  1. Dogs--Humor. I. Title.
  PN6231.D68T68 2005
  818'.602--dc22

                          2005008794

Distributed in Canada by Raincoast Books,
9050 Shaughnessy Street,
Vancouver, B.C. V6P 6E5

Published by Voyageur Press, Inc.
123 North Second Street, P.O. Box 338,
Stillwater, MN 55082 U.S.A.
651-430-2210, fax 651-430-2211
books@voyageurpress.com
www.voyageurpress.com

"Be still like a mountain and flow like a great river."

—LAO-TZU, FOUNDER OF TAOISM

THERE IS PERHAPS no creature in the world that embodies the Taoist philosophy more than the dog. Dogs have an innate ability to ignore time, exist in the moment, go with the flow, and just "be."

Take a typical day in a dog's life as a case and point: sleep on the bed, look out the window, sleep on the couch, lick paws, lick _____, move to sunny spot to sleep, get a drink of water, yawn, stretch, sleep…

To the untrained eye, it may look as if the dog just sleeps all day. Some may even go so far as to say the dog is a lazy animal. But what the unenlightened fail to recognize is that the many naps a dog takes during the day are actually times of self-centering meditation and contemplation, a place where dog and squeaky toy become one. It is while the dog is in this relaxed state of mind that he finds the answers to life's most perplexing questions: When will I get fed? Is it time for a walk? Where do squirrels live?

It seems, then, that humans, who have tried for eons to obtain peace with their place in the universe, could learn everything they need to know by taking a few moments to observe the humble hound. The following pages contain the finer lessons of dogma, the golden rules of the canine existence, as it were. Let *Bow Wow Tao* be the first step on your journey to enlightenment as you embark on the path of the pooch.

Direction gives life **clarity.**

ABOVE: A Pointer on point in a Midwestern field. (Photograph © J. C. Allen & Sons, Inc.)

FACING PAGE: A farm dog searches a corn shuck for critters in this quaint painting from a 1953 International Harvester calendar.

The search for **enlightenment** often leads to strange and mysterious places.

Peace with yourself
leads to peace with the **world.**

Children enjoy a lazy afternoon on the farm with their
canine companion in this 1953 calendar illustration.

Never let a **good day** go to waste.

A boy and his Collie daydream in this painting by Anthony Cucchi. The image, called *Shepherd of the Hills*, appeared on the cover of the October 1939 issue of the *Progressive Farmer*.

You don't know a man until you've walked a mile in his boots.

A puppy snuggles into a farmhand's work boot. (Photograph © J. C. Allen & Sons, Inc.)

Why walk when you can ride?

Proud owners pose for a photo with their favorite pup.

Judge not, lest thee be judged.

Judges size up the finer qualities of this hunting dog as canine enthusiasts look on.

Every **dog** has its **day**.

A Terrier gets chauffeured through the garden during an afternoon of play.
(Photograph © Library of Congress, Prints & Photographs Division)

Every dog
deserves to be
put up on a
pedestal.

A young girl is happy to
stand beside her two best
friends in this 1923 photograph.

The **heart's song** needs no audience.

A farm hound bays to his heart's content. (Photograph © J. C. Allen & Sons, Inc.)

Cuteness
is its own
reward.

Terriers are reliably cute.

It's better to be born a **beggar** than a **fool.**

A White Collie on an Indiana farm is well versed in the subtleties of obtaining a bite to eat. (Photograph © J. C. Allen & Sons, Inc.)

We **all** put on our pants **one leg** at a time.

LEFT: Vaudeville performer Syd Seymour includes an abiding Terrier in his act.

To err is **human**, to forgive, **canine.**

FACING PAGE: In this colorful painting by Walter Ohlson that appeared on the May 1940 cover of *Wee Wisdom* magazine, a playful pup toys with the clean laundry.

The **dog wags** its tail not for you,
but **for your bread.**

The whole family eagerly awaits a holiday dinner in this vintage painting
from a 1953 International Harvester calendar.

A **biscuit** a day keeps the doctor away.

Dogs nurse a friend back to health in this quirky, vintage French postcard.

Make sure to **keep** all your pups **in a row.**

A litter of hounds lines up for a photo . . . and perhaps a treat. (Photograph © J. C. Allen & Sons, Inc.)

Don't put **all** your puppies in **one** basket.

A young lad has his hands full with a litter of English Cocker Spaniel pups.
(Photograph © J. C. Allen & Sons, Inc.)

The bearer of good news
reaps the reward.

A young woman shares some good news with her dog, Rags. (Photograph © J. C. Allen & Sons, Inc.)

Don't believe
everything you hear.

A trustworthy canine graces the cover of the
March 1938 issue of *Dogs & Gossip* magazine.

Castles made of sand fall in the sea, eventually.

FACING PAGE: A young girl and her dog watch helplessly as a sand castle crumbles. The painting, by Walter Ohlson, appeared on the July 1940 issue of *Wee Wisdom* magazine.

A dog's house is his castle.

ABOVE: Yellow Labs relax at their home in Montana. (Photograph © Alan and Sandy Carey)

An ounce of **prevention** is worth a pound of **cure.**

This poor dog looks a little uncomfortable with his weight! (Photograph © J. C. Allen & Sons, Inc.)

It's weigh-in time in this painting by J. Knowles Hare that was featured on the January 1927 issue of *American Magazine*.

Puppies are **worth** their weight **in gold.**

A **good dog** deserves a good bone.

A Yellow Lab patiently waits for her master to reward her with the treat she has so carefully balanced on her snout. (Photograph © Karl Pearson-Cater)

Tongues have no bones,
but many a tongue has broken bones.

A Pomeranian wags her tongue. (Photograph © J. C. Allen & Sons, Inc.)

Share and **share alike.**

LEFT: A young girl and her dog share a rain cape in this Walter Ohlson illustration that appeared on the April 1941 issue of *Wee Wisdom* magazine.

Trouble shared is trouble halved.
Joy shared is joy doubled.

FACING PAGE: Gordon Ray Myers and Martha Charlene Allen cuddle with two young German Shepherds that are in training to become police dogs. (Photograph © J. C. Allen & Sons, Inc.)

Patience is a virtue

...**especially** when waiting for master to return home.

FACING PAGE: A boy and his best friend count the days until they can open gifts. This painting by Hy Hintermeister appeared on the December 1934 issue of the *Country Gentleman*.

BELOW: A loyal pooch waits patiently on the porch for its owner to arrive.

A cheerful heart
matches a cheerful countenance.

Monty, the English Bloodhound, wears a most sorrowful expression.

The way to a **dog's heart** is through its **stomach.**

It's time to break for lunch in this idyllic painting that appeared in a 1953 International Harvester calendar.

To appreciate **art** is to appreciate the **canine.**

An autumnal scene from a 1952
International Harvester calendar.

Fine **fellowship** makes a meal a **feast.**

Four hound puppies belly up to the bowl. (Photograph © J. C. Allen & Sons, Inc.)

A glove
without a match is like a dog without a **bone**.

The Saint Bernard was originally a rescue dog, saving many a stranded traveler in the snowy Swiss Alps.

Beauty is in the eye of the **beholder**.

How the photographer got these dogs to pose for this image we may never know. (Photograph © J. C. Allen & Sons, Inc.)

"**Outside** of a dog, a book is a man's best friend. **Inside** of a dog, it's too dark to read."

–GROUCHO MARX

A girl and her dog read a book in this vintage advertisement for McLaughlin's Coffee.

You **can** teach an old dog **new tricks.**

A farm dog learns the ins and outs of changing a bike tire in this painting from a 1953 International Harvester calendar.

When the **pupil** is ready, the **teacher** will come.

A Basset Hound puppy takes a lesson from a Rottweiler-Lab mix. (Photograph © Alan and Sandy Carey)

Still tryin'
to make both ends meet!

Often the **simplest goal**
requires the greatest effort.

A Dachshund chases its tail on this vintage postcard from 1909.

Great accomplishments come with **great** effort.

The dog on this campy colorized postcard needs a rest after a busy night.

Always **stand up** for what you believe.

LEFT: Duke the Hero-Dog saves the day in this 1942 children's book.

The world needs both **leaders** **and followers.**

FACING PAGE: Little Miss Molly walks her dog in a 1923 advertisement for silverware that appeared in the *Farmer's Wife* magazine.

We all need someone to **watch over us**.

A Pointer stands watch over a sleeping baby on the March 1938 cover of *Dogs & Gossip* magazine.

Chase a **cat** up a tree
and expect to be **scratched.**

A stealthlike Terrier contemplates his next move. (Photograph © J. C. Allen & Sons, Inc.)

If you ask no **questions,** you shall hear no lies.

LEFT: In this 1923 illustration from the *Farmer's Wife* magazine, a young hunter and his dog look sorry to have trespassed on private property.

Keep a **spring** in your step and a **dog** at your heels and **happiness** will follow.

FACING PAGE: These kids couldn't have asked for a better day for a picnic! The illustration is by Walter Ohlson, and it appeared on the cover of the August 1941 issue of *Wee Wisdom* magazine.

Take time each day to
commune with nature.

On the shores of Lake Superior, Jack the Beagle contemplates the meaning of life. (Photograph © Brian I. Cornell)

A bird in the **mouth** is worth two in the **bush**.

A Springer Spaniel returns from the hunt with a prized pheasant. This illustration, by J. F. Kernan, appeared on the cover of the November 1934 issue of *Country Gentleman* magazine.

Good
things come in **small**
packages.

Jerry Mathers, star of the 1950s TV show *Leave it to Beaver,* cuddles his pet Chihuahua.

Sometimes a
big hug
is all you need.

An English Bloodhound
is a great comfort to this
little girl.

Everyday is an opportunity to **give** of yourself.

Saint Bernards prepare to haul a milk cart in this vintage Swiss postcard.

A dog's work is **never** done.

A man and his dog, loaded down with camp supplies, are ready to head into the Alaskan wilderness.

Nothing beats a good **nap** after a hard day's **work.**

A dedicated hunting dog settles down for a snooze alongside his master's gun and the recent catch.

Let **sleeping** dogs lie.

A Golden Retriever puppy sleeps soundly after tangling with a rope.
(Photograph © Alan and Sandy Carey)

You're never alone when you're
among friends.

LEFT: A gang of Golden Retrievers wonder if there will be treats once the photo is taken. (Photograph © Janis Leventhal)

The reason a dog has so many friends is that he wags **his tail** instead of **his tongue.**

FACING PAGE: A young girl sits proudly beside her Collie puppy. (Photograph © J. C. Allen & Sons, Inc.)

Vary your **friends** and vary your **outlook**.

BELOW: A Golden Retriever and a cat appear to be gossiping about someone in the distance. (Photograph © J. C. Allen & Sons, Inc.)

A dog is known by the **company** he keeps.

FACING PAGE: This loyal farm dog stays close to his master's side. (Photograph © J. C. Allen & Sons, Inc.)

Gracefully accepting **admiration** is the path to **humility**.

Love
is a many splendored thing.

LEFT: A young girl snuggles with two new pups. (Photograph © J. C. Allen & Sons, Inc.)

FACING PAGE: Children shower their dog with affection in this 1930s photograph. (Photograph © Bruce Sifford Studio, used courtesy of the Minnesota Historical Society)

Don't **worship** false gods.

A Terrier gazes fondly at a photo of a beloved ancestor. (Photograph ©
Library of Congress, Prints & Photographs Division)

Absence makes the heart **grow fonder**.

Kids leave mom and the family dog behind as they board the bus for school. This quaint painting originally appeared in a 1953 International Harvester calendar.

Friends help smooth life's bumpy roads.

A young hunter prepares his dog for the task at hand.

Working like a dog is **hardly** working.

ABOVE: Sparky the fire dog cruises in his fire truck on the cover of this 1955 coloring book.

Cleanliness is next to **dogliness.**

Ahh, there's nothing better than a good scrubbing in the ol' wash tub.
(Photograph © J. C. Allen & Sons, Inc.)

Beauty is only
fur deep.

A content dog owner poses
for a photo with her best
friend on the front steps of
their California home.

Pulling your own weight is a **virtue,**
but pulling the weight of others is **saintly.**

A little girl in fancy dress tours the gardens in a cart pulled by the family sheep dog. (Photograph © Fred Hultstrand "History in Pictures" Collection, NDSU, Fargo, ND)

Sharing the load makes the load light.

Two hard-working dogs pull their masters through the snow. (Photograph © Fred Hultstrand "History in Pictures" Collection, NDSU, Fargo, ND)

It's always a good idea to befriend a few fellows who are **bigger** than you.

A trip to the park for this little boy wouldn't be the same without his closest companion.

You're never **too big** for a little cuddling.

Maybe so, but this Mastiff threatens to collapse his master's flimsy lawn chair.

Love freely given is love gained.

A young boy holds his two Collie puppies close.
(Photograph © J. C. Allen & Sons, Inc.)

Take time to stop and smell the flowers . . .
but don't eat them!

A Scottish Terrier munches on a gladiolus on this July 1934 cover of the *Country Home* magazine.

Keep your **friends close** and your **enemies closer.**

A farm cat shares a secret with a Labrador mix. (Photograph © J. C. Allen & Sons, Inc.)

You can't put a price on **happiness.**

This idyllic scene, painted by Walter Haskell Hinton, appeared in a 1959 calendar.

The **best** things in life are **free**.

A farm kid takes a break with his favorite farmhand. (Photograph © J. C. Allen & Sons, Inc.)

Never forget the **one you love.**

When the family goes horseback riding, the dog is never far behind. This colorful Walter Ohlson painting appeared on the cover of the August 1942 issue of *Wee Wisdom* magazine.

A **trusty sidekick** is hard to find.

Looks as if cowboy-actor Roy Rogers has found a keeper.

There's no place like **home**.

With a bone in the bowl and his name over the door, this is one pampered pooch.

Mi casa es su casa.

A kitchy postcard from the 1950s.

A **home**
is where you
make it.

A scruffy canine hangs out at home.

Good fences

make good neighbors.

Young and old exchange tips on raising the perfect pup. (Photograph © J. C. Allen & Sons, Inc.)

Friendship is **one** mind with **two** bodies.

LEFT: This boy and his dog share the same smile. (Photograph © J. C. Allen & Sons, Inc.)

Happiness is a warm **puppy.**

FACING PAGE: A Dachshund pup finds safety in the arms of 1930s film star Jean Harlowe.

Be **patient** and some day
your **ship** will come in.

A pair of Newfoundlands stand watch in this painting by
Louis Agassiz Fuertes.

Grasp life with all four paws.

A dog with an adventurous spirit surfs with his master at Waikiki Beach in the 1930s. (Photograph © Hawaii State Archives)

A Scotch Collie has a fence-side chat with a couple of pals. (Photograph © J. C. Allen & Sons, Inc.)

Keep your feet on the **ground** but keep reaching for the **stars.**